SOAP MAKING
FOR BEGINNERS

TABLE OF CONTENTS

Introduction 1

Chapter 1: The Basics of Making Your Own Soap 3

    The methods of soap making 4

        The cold process method 5

        The hot process 7

        Melt and pour method 9

    Which method is the right one for me 11

Chapter 2: What Ingredients Do I Need to Get Started? 13

    The tools 13

        Staying safe while using lye 14

    The equipment needed to make soap 16

    Choosing your mold 18

    Picking out the type of fat you would like to use 19

    Picking out the lye you will use 21

    Other things to add into the soap 21

    Making Soaps to Sell 24

Chapter 3: Some of the Benefits of Making My Own Soap 27

Chapter 4: Some Easy Recipes to Get You Started 31

Conclusion 45

INTRODUCTION

How many times have you headed to the store to buy some soap for your family, or any other beauty product, and just felt frustrated at the selection that you saw there? You most likely saw that there were only a handful of options to choose from in the first place, and most of them were boring with no great scents or colors or make them fun. If you have a skin allergy to an ingredient that is inside of most soaps, the process of finding any soap to use can become more frustrating than before.

This guidebook is going to give you a solution to all of this. Rather than having to rely on the store bought brands of soap, you will be able to pick from a wide variety of options that you can make from home. Inside this guidebook, we are going to spend some time talking about how you can make some of your own soaps at home and have a great time doing it.

We will start off this guidebook with some of the basics of making your own soaps. We will talk about some of the processes that are commonly used at home, such as the cold process, the hot process and the melt and pour process, that help you to make some of your own soaps. Once we are done with that, we will move on to talk more about some of the utensils that you need to make some of your soaps, and how you need to also be careful with the products used to ensure that some, like the lye, don't cause skin irritation while designing the soaps.

Next, we will move on to talking about some of the benefits that come with making your own soaps at home, such as being able to save money, having more options over what goes in the soap, and how it is even safer for you to use. And finally, this guidebook will end with a chapter of some of the best soap recipes that you can use, that are easy to make and also safe on the skin.

Making some of your own soaps at home can be a really rewarding experience. This guidebook is going to give you the basics that you need to get started, even if you don't have experience with doing this in the past. Take a look through this guidebook and see what all you are able to learn about making your own personal soaps at home.

CHAPTER 1:

THE BASICS OF MAKING YOUR OWN SOAP

When it comes to making your own soap, there are a few methods that you will be able to use. The nice thing is that the chemical process of each of these methods is going to be pretty similar. You will start out by getting a fat and then treating it with an alkaline solution; the method you use to treat the fat will vary depending on the type of products used and the recipe you are going with. Sometimes you will do this by mixing the alkaline solution and the fat together, and other times you will boil together the ingredients before extracting the soap out of the water.

This chemical process is going to be known as saponification. During this process, the fatty acids that are attached to your fats are going to become loose and then reform together into a new substance. This new substance is going to be a combination of glycerin, salts, alkali, and fats. All of these are useful for binding the soap together, helping the body to feel extra moisture and exfoliation, and so much more.

The best ingredient that stays inside the soap when you make it on your own is the glycerin. With most manufactured soaps, this is the first ingredient to go because it is hard to keep in the mixture. The result is that most soaps are missing out on all the moisturizers that come with glycerin, and dry skin and other skin disorders are the ones that will suffer the most.

In addition to adding in the basic alkaline solution and the fat, you can choose to add in some scents in the form of perfumes or the different colors that you would like. These are not required so if you would like to keep things simple and just want to get some of the benefits that come from homemade soap, this would be fine to work with as well. There are so many options that come with making some of your own soap at home that once you give it a try, you will never want to go back to the store bought brands.

The methods of soap making

When it comes to making your own soap, there are actually many different processes that you can use to get it done. But for the most part, people are going to choose from the two main options: the cold method or the hot method. Both of these are going to work to combine together the fat and the alkali, but the method that they use to get the water to leave the mixture so that you just get the soap is going to be slightly different. Let's take a look at the different types of soap making that you can choose so that you can choose the one that is right for you.

The cold process method

First we will take a look at the cold method. This one is pretty simple, but you will have to pay more attention to it compared to the hot method because it requires more precision. To get started with this method, you will need to pick up the fat and then look to see what the saponification value is of that fat. This is basically the amount of alkali that you will need to use in order to begin treating the fat to make it into soap. Some fats are going to need higher amounts of lye while others would just need a little bit. Your recipe will often make this easier by telling you how much of each product you will need.

One interesting thing to keep in mind is that if you have ever used a soap that felt too itchy or had one that seemed to fall apart, this means that the pH was too high for your skin. Each person is going to have a different amount of pH that they are able to handle, which is why some people are going to be more sensitive to the things they put on their bodies while others would be just fine. The nice thing is that you will get some more control over how much lye will be in the soap. If you are sensitive to this ingredient, you will be able to cut it out a bit and keep the soap healthy for you.

There also needs to be a bit of a balancing act when it comes to making these though. While you may want to cut out the lye amount that is in your soap, if you place in too much of the fat, and leave out the lye too much, then the soap can get greasy and it may not set the right way inside of your soap. Usually people will try to add in some more of the fat than is recommended because it is better to have the soap be a bit greasy than to have the irritated skin that comes from too much alkaline, but you should try to find the balance that is right for you.

To do the cold method, you need to make sure that the lye and the fat are in their liquid form. If they are solid, you will need to melt the fat to make it a liquid and you can dissolve the lye in some water before pouring them together and stirring to make the ingredients emulsified and the mixture is thick. Yes, you will need to use a bit of heat to get the fat into a liquid form, but you will never need to heat up the soap, hence the reason for being able to call this the cold method.

At this point, you can also add in the dyes and the scents that you want to use into your soap, but as you get used to the process, you will be able to pick the time that is right for you. You will then find the mold that you want to use for the soap, pour the mixture inside and leave this in a location where it is left alone for at least a day. Cover this up with a towel to ensure that nothing gets in and ruins the soap.

After some time as passed, the soap should be firm and you will be able to remove it from the mold. Now you are able to start using it in the manner that you would like, or you can store it the right way to make sure that the soap stays good for as long as you need.

The cold method is the one that most people who make their own soaps at home will use. It is a simple process that works well and it isn't going to be that expensive. You will just need to pick out the fat and the lye that you would like to use, along with some of the extras if you choose to go with them, and then bring out a mold that you would be able to use for a long time to make the high quality soap. In addition, this method is going to leave in some of the extra glycerin, which is perfect for those who want to add in that extra moisture.

The downside to using the cold method is that if you mess up with the mixture, it is easier to make this soap more harmful than using the hot method. Luckily, this is a small concern and after some practice, the soap is going to come out fine each time. Also, this method is a bit slower to make because you have to wait so long to make the soap get hard, but if you have some time to wait, it isn't that bad.

The hot process

Now that you know a bit about using the cold method, it is time to move on to the hot method of making soaps. In this method, you are making the saponification process go so much faster than before. This can make it easier to get the soap done if you are in a hurry, and you will be able to use the soap pretty quickly after you are done.

Just like you did with the cold method, you will need to bring out the lye and the fat of your choice and then place them into a pot. Turn this on to a medium high setting (you can adjust it later on based on how your stove works and how much heat the process needs). After your mixture has the time to turn into a thick gel, you will notice that the saponification is taking place.

Now this gel stage is something that happens with the cold method, but it is going to happen while it is inside the mold and sitting around for a few days. But with the hot method, you will be able to see it happen in front of you. This is the stage where you are going to add in the perfumes and the dyes that you want to have with the soap. After all the extra ingredients are added in, you will be able to pour this into the mold that you would want to use. You will need to wait for some time to get the soap to cool down before you cut it out of the mold and let it finish drying before using.

When you work with the hot process method, you are not going to have to worry about the mixture because the heating is going to make it so that the saponification will happen and it will enter the gel phase right away, right in front of your eyes, something that is hard to tell with the cold method. The heating phase is also going to make it easier to see that the additives to the soap, such as the dyes and the scents, won't do anything to mess with the forming process.

With the cold method, you also have to worry about some of the oils that you add in becoming neutered. This is because they are placed into the mixture before the saponification process, meaning that they are going to go through this process as well. But when you are working with the hot method, the oils and dyes are going to come in just at the end of the process, after the saponification process is done, so they should be just find.

Another thing to note is that if you would like to make liquid hand soap, especially if you would like it to be colorless, you will want to go with the hot method rather than with the cold. This makes it easier to remove the glycerin when you are working with the hot method, and you will get some amazing hand soap for your needs.

Melt and pour method

While the cold method and the hot method are the most common types that you will use when working in soap making, there is a third option that is known as the melt and pour method. With this one, you would take some pre-made soap and then melt it on the stove on a medium high heat. Once that has melted down, you will be able to add in some of the extra dyes and scents that you would like into the mixture and then pour into the molds that you want.

Since this is going to be done with some soap that is already made, you will not have to worry about using either of the methods that we discussed above. You will just need to melt down the soap and then add in the other ingredients that you would like before placing into a mold and letting it set.

There are a few benefits to using this method. First, you will find that if you just want to experiment a bit with the soap making process and you don't plan to make a ton of the soap to have around, this method is going to end up being about the same but it is so much easier. In addition, you won't have to worry about handling lye and going with all the safety equipment that this usually needs. You will basically just need a jug and the mold that you would like, along with any scents and colors to add to the soap.

But while this may be a good method to use when you are first learning how to make soaps and it can be easy, it is not always the best option to go with. First, it isn't going to make the best soap. You are basically taking the same soap that you didn't like in the first place and just adding a few things to it. You will still have to deal with the same soap without any of the added benefits of getting good ingredients inside of it.

You will also find that if you would like to make a lot of soap as a present to or have on hand for your own needs, this is going to be a more expensive method compared to just making it all on your own. Your soaps aren't going to have the same fat choices inside of them, you are going to be limited to the types of soaps that you did in the past, and it just won't result in the same kind of result that you want.

For the most part, unless you want to get a bit of experience and you have some of the traditional soap sitting around your home, you will probably not want to go with the melt and pour method. It seems better, but you may as well go with some of your older options of soap. The other two methods are not going to be that hard to accomplish, and you will enjoy that they are easy to make and have a lot more options and benefits compared to your melt and pour method.

Which method is the right one for me

There is no straightforward answer to this question. It is going to depend on what you would like out of the soap making process, and it also changes based on which one you feel is the best for you. If you would like to make soaps pretty quickly, then the hot method is going to be the best option because you will be able to create the large batches of soap in just a few days and there aren't as many issues of combining the chemicals correctly. You will also find that the hot method is the best when working on liquid hand soaps.

On the other hand, most beginners find that the cold method is the best for them, especially if they choose to just make a small amount of soap. You will not need as many parts to make the soap and you won't have to leave the lye mixture sitting around for a few hours. Preparing the molds for the soaps inside the cold process is easy, and you will not have to worry about the water becoming too hot and evaporating the oils that you are doing. In addition, the cold process is better when you want to have opaque solid soaps, or ones that are lighter in color because the process is more suited to the cold method rather than to the hot method.

Basically, the method that you choose is going to be based on what you would like to have happen with your soap. Some of the methods work better for certain types of soaps, and sometimes beginners will find that the method of cold process is going to be the best for them. You can try these out a few times and learn which one works the best for your needs, depending on your methods of creating soaps, and which one you prefer.

CHAPTER 2:

WHAT INGREDIENTS DO I NEED TO GET STARTED?

Now that we have taken some time to look at the various parts of creating your own soap, including some of the things that you will need and an explanation of all the different types of methods that you can use in order to make soaps, it is time to work on some of the ingredients that you will need in order to get started. The ingredients that you will need often vary based on the type of soap that you would like to create, if you would like to add in any dyes to make a color, and what scents would be preferable for you. Let's take a look at some of the tools and ingredients that you will need in order to get started with creating your own soaps.

The tools

It is probably not the best to make your soaps inside of cooking pots and other items that you will need to use in order to prepare food in later. You may find that some of the soap will get left behind when you are done and this can be an unsanitary way to make your food in the future. This is why most people who decide to make their own soaps will get some new containers in order to get the process done and to ensure that everything stays safe. If you have some older pots that you are no longer using, these will work great or purchase some second hand items that won't cost you as much.

Staying safe while using lye

In addition to having to make sure that you have the right cleaning tools as well as the right pots and pans, you are going to need a few ingredients on hand to make your soap. One of these ingredients is the alkaline material, or the lye. You need to take some extra caution when it comes to working with lye, especially when you are making it together with your fat. You will find that if lye gets onto your skin or on your clothes, it could end up being corrosive, depending on the amount that gets on you. It also isn't going to be the easiest to wash off with water, which could make it all the more dangerous.

Let's take a look at the problem with lye. When you look at your skin, you will notice that it has a pH that is around 7. If you get something that is high on the pH scale, it is going to try to find equilibrium by raising the level of the pH on the skin. Lye is known for eating oils and fats and it can also dissolve the proteins that are in your skin. It also has a really high pH that is near 14.

If you do get lye on your bare skin, it is important to quickly get the pH to come down. Soap is going to have lye inside of it so this is not the best one for you to use because it will be higher than what is on your skin. In addition, the water in your sink is going to be 7, the same as your skin so using that is going to end up with the same result as leaving the lye sit there on the skin.

A good option to go with is to find an acid. White vinegar is a good option if you are able to find it in your pantry. White vinegar has a pH that is 2 and in theory, you should be able to neutralize the lye a bit. The best bet to avoid issues is to just keep the lye off of your skin when you are making soap.

There are a number of things that you are able to do to avoid getting the lye on you or on your clothes. When you are working with the lye, it is a good idea to cover up as much of your skin as you can, such as wearing long sleeve shirts to be safe. You will need to use some caution any time that you are near the lye to avoid getting some of the splashes on you. Some people want to have some extra precautions with the lye and will choose to wear a face mask of some kind. If you are in an area that is well ventilated and you mix in enough water with the lye, the mask is not that necessary, but you may want to have one just in case. As a side note, make sure that you are always adding in the lye to the water and not the other way around.

The biggest issue that you are going to find when you are dealing with lye isn't going to happen when you are using the lye, it is going to be during the storage and cleaning up period after you have taken off the protective gear. You need to bring out a vinegar based cleaner and clean down any surface that the lye may have touched during the soap making process. You should also make sure that the lye solution is stored and closed up as tightly as possible, and that you keep them away from children inside a plastic container.

When you are picking out the container that you are going to use with lye, you should be careful about using a container that is metal. Metal is going to work with the lye in order to make a chemical reaction as soon as the lye meets together with the water, so keeping this in a plastic bowl is one of the best bets. If you happen to handle these soap mixtures later on, you should make sure to wear your protective gear. Once it is hardened and you have time to let it cure a bit, you will be able to touch it and not worry about the lye any longer.

The equipment needed to make soap

So far we have talked about using lye and how you should be careful about having it in your mixture, and about the used pots and pans and other equipment that is needed to get the heating process, and the other processes done while making soap. When it comes to picking out the rest of the equipment that you need, you should make sure that you have some spoons, as well as some stirrers to watch the mixtures with. You should have these be plastic or metal, and then bring along a spatula so that you are able to scrape the mixture over to the molds when it is all done.

When you want to stir together the water and the lye, you will need to bring along a pitcher and a jug that are made out of either plastic or glass. You should make sure that it is pretty big - big enough to contain all the mixture with a bit of room left so that it doesn't spill when you are mixing. You will also need to have a good scale that will help to measure out the lye, so that you are able to get it to be accurate. You can also use this scale to help measure out the amount of fat that you would like to add in.

When it comes to the oils and the fats that you are using inside of your soaps, you will probably need to use some dishes and some pans, but make sure that you don't use them for anything other than making soap so that you don't end up making anyone sick. When you are ready to mix together the lye and fat, you will need to use a large glass or metal pot or a big glass pitcher, just make sure that they are big enough to hold the ingredients that you have.

A hand blender can be useful at times when you want to stir the ingredients of the soap together and any other times, but make sure that you are using them just for the soap so that you avoid any cross-contamination.

While this may seem like it is going to be an expensive process just to get the tools that you need to make the soap, it really isn't that bad. You will be able to find a lot of these items in your own home in the form of old items that you aren't even using any more. If you do need to get a brand new item, take a look at some of the thrift stores in your area to find some of these products for a lower cost, and some of them may be almost new. Make sure to store these in the proper place so that you only use them when you are creating soap and no other times.

Choosing your mold

The next step that you will need to work with is picking out the mold. These are going to be the containers that you place the soap in so that they have some time to cool down. You can pick a simple one that is going to place the soap in the shape of a simple bar like you will find at the store, or you can pick out a mold that is a bit unique and offers some other options. There are a few things that you are going to have to consider when picking out your mold, including the following:

First, you should consider how you will be able to get the soap form out of the mold. Some molds are designed to make it easy to get the mold right out without any issues, but others may make this a challenge. Do you really want to spend a lot of your time trying to get the soap to come out of the mold when it is all done? Make sure to check the mold and see if it seems set up to make things easy for getting the finished soaps out.

The second thing that you should consider is the shape that you would like the finished soaps to be. If you would like to keep this simple, you will be able to choose a simple mold that is just in the shape of the bar soap that you see inside the stores. Other times you may want to go with a unique option like a fish, a heart, or something else. There are often groups of molds that are all different shapes but sold together to make this easier to pick from and to change things up when needed.

And finally, you will need to make sure that you are looking at the price that comes with your molds. Some of these are going to be too cheap and will all apart the first time that you use them, but others are going to be too expensive for your budget, especially if you aren't sure if you will keep up with making soaps. You can often find some good quality molds that will fit your budget as long as you set a price from the beginning and take some time to look around for the right one.

Picking out the type of fat you would like to use

As we have mentioned a bit inside of this guidebook, you are going to need some kind of fat in order to make the soap. These fats are going to help to hold the soap together and if you choose the right one, they can help to provide some added benefit to your body. There are many options when it comes to the types of fats that you are able to use in your soaps, and some of the most common ones that you can choose from include:

- Lard and tallow: these are good for all around soaps that won't have a lot of other things added to them. They are going to give a lather that is creamy and they are going to be good at cleaning. Be aware that they are often going to produce a milky color and sometimes you will want to balance them out by using a conditioning fat.

- Cocoa butter and shea butter: these are going to make some creamy soaps that bring about a good lather. They are not the best for cleaning up, but they will make a hard soap that is going to last for a long time.
- Sunflower, avocado, castor, rapeseed, and olive oil: this list of oils are going to help out with their cleaning and lather abilities, but the lather is going to be a bit lower than some of the other options. They have a lot of good conditioning properties, and they are good to balance out the damage that comes with some of the drying soaps.
- Coconut oil and palm kernel oil: these are the oils that are really good for cleaning things up and they are going to add in a ton of bubbles to the soap. Keep in mind that if you add in too many of these to the skin, they are going to dry out the skin.
- Jojoba oil and beeswax: these are the oils that are going to reduce the lather found inside of the soap and they are considered very waxy. If you would like to make out some soaps that are hard and will last for a long time on the shelf, but you should add in some other fats if you would like to get some more of the moisture and benefits.

As you can see, there are quite a few options that come with picking out the right fat that you will use inside of your soaps. Sometimes you may choose to combine a few of them together in order to get the benefits of both. For example, you may want to pick the oils that help with a long shelf life along with the ones that will clean the body well, so that you get the best of both worlds inside your soap.

Picking out the lye you will use

In addition to having to pick out the type of fat that you want to place into the soap, you will need to take some time to pick out the lye that you will use. In some areas, it is a bit difficult to find the lye that you would like to use. You are not able to go out and pick up any type of lye that you come across. There are some that are better for making into soap and some that are better for working on some other projects.

You will want to make sure that the type of lye that you are using is pretty much completely lye. You will not need to go with 100 percent, 98 to 99 percent can be just as good, but it should be one of the purest forms that you can have. It is best to stick with the sodium hydroxide powder rather than going with any mixes or solutions that have lye inside of them because you never know what has been added. Shopping online is often the best choice because you will be able to ask questions and find out whether the lye is going to be the best one for making your soap projects.

Other things to add into the soap

Basically, you are going to be fine if you choose to just add in a few fats and the lye to your soap. This is going to be enough to keep you clean and provide a nice lather without adding a ton of cost to the whole project. Of course, if you are choosing to make some of your own soaps at home, you are more than likely looking to add in some more variety when it comes to your options, and being able to add in some scents and some colors is a great way to do it.

Many essential oils as well as different spices are going to be great for adding in a bit of a scent to your soap. You will be able to take a look at your recipe and find out all the options that are available for making this soap smell the way that you want. If you are going the route of working in aromatherapy with the scents that you use, make sure to do your research and find out which scents are going to not only work well inside of the soap, but will work for whatever condition you are trying to deal with.

In addition, you are able to choose to add in some colors to the soap that you are making. You should choose to go with natural forms of coloring because they are really going to provide a deep color, one of the best that you can find inside of a soap, and they are not going to drain off and make the bath tub water a silly color. Experiment a bit to see which colors are going to be the best for some of the soaps that you are using.

For those who are interested in adding in some of the other things to your soaps, there are going to be a lot of great essential oils that you will be able to use. Make sure that you aren't putting in so much of these that you aren't able to get the benefits from the fat and the alkaline substance that you are using inside of your product, but adding in a few drops here and there can make the scents so much better and will help you to enjoy your bath more than you were in the past.

Essential oils are one of the best options to use for scents because they are the most powerful and you will be able to get away with just using a few drops and still getting the scent that you want. Some people choose to use fresh or dried herbs and spices to do this work as well. These can be incredible inside the soap, but keep in mind they are not as strong as the essential oils and will take more of the product to get the scent that you want.

In addition, you may want to add in some of the colors to your product. Colors can make it fun for kids or make it an even better idea for gift giving to your friends and family. If you are going to use coloring in your soaps, try to find some that are specific for soap making. If you choose the wrong kind, you could end up with a mess all over your hands and in the tub, but the soap making variety are often the best and will help you to get some better results that you want.

As you get more advanced with your soap making capabilities, you will find that there are a lot of other things that you are able to add inside of the soaps you are making. You could add in some little scrubbing agents, add in some cool designs, or even a nice little toy to make it more fun for the people you would like to give them to (or to sell them to if this is the route you are planning on going with). There are just so many options when it comes to making some of your own soaps, and as you advance and get more used to doing these, you will find that it can be a lot of fun.

Making soap can be a fun and rewarding experience for everyone to enjoy. You will be able to add in some more options than you would with the choices that are at the store and you will enjoy that they are simple enough to make. Just make sure that you are picking out the right ingredients in your home to make the soaps, without sharing them with other processes you do in the home such as cooking, and you are sure to get some of the best results possible when making your own soaps.

Making Soaps to Sell

One thing that is becoming popular for a lot of people to work with is to design their own soaps in order to sell them to other people. There are a lot of people who are looking for homemade soaps for their own personal use or to give it as a present to someone they care about. But these people either don't have the time to create some of these products on their own, they have no interest in doing so, or they just think that the process is going to be too complicated for them to complete. No matter the reason, you will be able to capitalize on this need and make some money on the side.

If you do decide to sell some soaps on the side, you will need to add in a few more ingredients and supplies to make sure that the soaps are ready to sell. You may need to go with some special molds so that you can make a unique shape that others don't have. You may want to go with some essential oils and keep those in stock so that you can add in some new scents and aromatherapy that the customers would like. Anything unique that you are able to add into your soaps will really help them to stand out and for others to want to make a purchase of them instead of another seller.

In addition to needing to add something special to the soaps that you are making, you will also need to take the time to have some packing supplies ready to go. If you could find a unique box or shipping container to send these out in rather than just the simple envelope that the post office has, you will really impress the customer. You may want to keep a few of these on hand to speed up the delivery process and to make the customer not have to wait too long in order to get their soaps.

If you would like to have some other special features of the soap, such as some more great packaging that will impress your customers, you need to keep some of those supplies around the house as well. You could waste a lot of time going out each time that you have an order just to get some of the supplies that you need. But when it comes to selling soaps, you will want to be efficient and make sure that you are keeping all of your supplies on hand for right when you need them the most.

Keep in mind that these are all extras that you are able to deal with if you want to really see some results with selling your soaps. If you plan to just use your soaps for your own personal needs, all this extra stuff is not as important as it would be with selling. When it comes to selling, you need to make sure that your presentation is perfect and will impress other people, but when you are making them for your own, it doesn't matter as much so you will be able to get away with fewer supplies.

Making some of your own soaps can be a rewarding experience, and outside of waiting for the ingredients to set when you are working on the cold process method, it is not going to take that much of your time to make a ton of them. And since your costs are sure to be low and easy to handle, you are going to be able to make a good profit off the soaps that you are making, as long as you are able to follow some of the suggestions in this guidebook! The supplies you need will vary based on if you are making these soaps for your own personal use or if you are trying to sell them to other people, but the process and the amount of fun you will have will remain the same both times!

CHAPTER 3:

SOME OF THE BENEFITS OF MAKING MY OWN SOAP

When you need soap in your home, the first thing you usually do is head over to your local grocery store and get some of your favorite brand. The selections are often going to be limited and you may not be that happy with the options that you are going to get from here. There may be a few brands on there and each of them may have a couple of scents, depending on the area you are located, and then you are stuck. If you don't like the price or if you have an allergy that makes it hard to use the soaps that are available at your local store, it can be hard to find any soap that is going to work for your needs.

There are so many benefits that you will be able to enjoy when you are working on making your own soaps. You will enjoy that the price is so affordable, especially if you make these in bulk. You will like all the choices that you can get from making the soaps, including the ingredients, the process that you use, the colors, and even the scents. Some of the other benefits that you will be able to enjoy when you choose to make some of your own soaps at home include:

- Affordable: when you pick making soaps at home, you get to save a lot of money. You can make the soaps in bulk and see that making the bars of soap can be just a few cents each!
- Choose the scents: have you always wanted to add in a certain scent to the soaps that you are using, or you don't like the scents that come in the soaps at the store? Making your own soaps can help to solve this issue. You will be able to pick out the scent that is right for you without having to hope that it is available in the store.
- Avoid some bad ingredients: there are a lot of bad ingredients can be found inside of regular soap. Or, you may have a skin allergy to certain ingredients and finding soaps that don't have this ingredient could be difficult. When you make some of these soaps at home, you will find that you can avoid some of these bad ingredients. You will always know what is inside the soap you are making because you are the one who gets to pick out the ingredients.
- More variety: when you go to the store, you may notice that your options are pretty slim. You may only get one or two choices and then a couple different brands. While they may work for you, is it really that much fun to only have a few

options. When you make some of your own soaps at home, you can add in as much variety as you would like. You could choose to make them all the same kind of your favorite scent or color, or make a variety of batches that are all different and see how easy it is to mix and match together.

- Fun experience: if you need a fun activity for the whole family to enjoy at home, why not decide to make some soap together? You can get some fun molds and let everyone decide what kind of soap they would like to make. Let them pick from the shapes, the colors and the scents, and spend all afternoon having fun while making some great soaps for your needs.
- Safer: there are a lot of chemicals in the soap products, as well as other health and beauty products, on the market. If you looked at the ingredients, you may find that you can't even pronounce most of the names on the list. Some of these can be harmful to you, harmful to your family members, and even harmful to the environment. When you make some of your own soaps at home, you will find that the ingredients are safer and better for you to use.
- Can make money from them: if you are an entrepreneur and would like to make some extra money from home, you may find that making some of your own soaps and then selling them can be a great idea. You will find that a lot of people would like to have the benefits of homemade soaps for their

homes or for a gift, but they just don't have the time, or think it is too hard, to create any of their own soaps. This can be a great second income as long as you are able to find some unique combinations that will really entice people to choose your option over another one.

Making some of your own products at home, especially when it comes to making soap products, there are a lot of benefits that you will enjoy. You will like that it can save you a lot of money, you will be able to choose what goes inside of each of them, and that it is so much safer than just randomly picking out a soap product at the store.

CHAPTER 4:

SOME EASY RECIPES TO GET YOU STARTED

Velvet Raspberry Soap

Ingredients:

- 4 drops red soap coloring
- 6 drops raspberry oil
- 1 Tbsp. aloe vera gel
- 1 lb. unscented glycerin base

Directions:

1. Take out a few pans and melt the glycerin until it is smooth using the double broiler method.
2. When the glycerin is melted, add in the rest of the ingredients and mix them until smooth.
3. Pour this into a mold and place into the fridge to harden for 24 hours.
4. Use the soap right away or store until later.

Rosy Lavender

Ingredients:

- ½ tsp. rosemary oil
- 1 tsp. dry rosemary
- 1 ½ tsp. lavender oil
- ¼ c. oil with rosemary in it
- 3 c. unscented and clear glycerin base

Directions:

1. Take out a few pots and set up a double boiler. Place the glycerin inside this and let it heat up until it is completely melted.
2. Add in the rest of the ingredients and stir around so that they become nice and smooth.
3. Pour these into your chosen mold and then place in the fridge to set for the next 24 hours.
4. Use the soap when it is done.

Youth Almond Soap

Ingredients:

8 drops brown soap coloring
1 Tbsp. almond oil
40 drops patchouli essential oil
40 drops rose oil
16 oz. unscented and clear glycerin base

Directions:

1. Set up a double broiler with your pots and then place the glycerin inside. Let it heat up until it is melted and then remove.
2. Add in the rest of the ingredients into this and then stir until they are completely combined.
3. Bring out the mold of your choice and then pour the soap inside. Place into the fridge to set for the next 24 hours.
4. Use the soap when you are ready.

Apple Pie Scented Soap

Ingredients:

    2 drops pink soap coloring
    ½ tsp. cinnamon powder
    1 tsp. apple fragrance oil
    16 oz. clear glycerin base

Directions:

1. Take out the glycerin and place it into your prepared double boiler. Let this heat up until it is completely melted.
2. When the glycerin is done, you are able to add in your other ingredients and stir to combine.
3. Next, bring out the mold that you would like to use and then place it into the fridge to cool down and set for 24 hours.
4. When this is done, choose to use the soap or save it in a safe place for later.

Plantain Goodness Soap

Ingredients:

    2 Tbsp. plantain oil
    ¼ c. water
    ½ c. liquid glycerin
    4 c. unscented glycerin base

Directions:

1. Take out your double boiler and then place the glycerin liquid and the glycerin base inside. Let these come to a melting point.
2. Add in the rest of the ingredients once the glycerin has melted. Stir to combine them together well.
3. Pour this mixture into your chosen molds and then place into the fridge to cool down for the next 24 hours.
4. When these are done, you can use the soap right away!

Velvet Chamomile Soap

Ingredients:

    2 drops lavender oil
    2 drops rose oil
    4 drops chamomile oil
    Liquid from 3 vitamin E capsules
    2 tsp. rice bran oil
    3 Tbsp. aloe vera gel
    1 lb. unscented and white glycerin base

Directions:

1. Take out your double boiler and add the rice bran oil and the glycerin inside. Let these melt together until they are nice and smooth.
2. When those two ingredients are well combined, it is time to add in the rest of your ingredients and stir well.
3. Bring out the molds that you want to use and pour the soap mixture inside. Place into the fridge and let these harden for the next 24 hours.
4. When the soaps are done, bring them out and use them right away.

Velvet Cherry Soap

Ingredients:

8 drops rose oil
8 drops red soap coloring
24 drops cherry oil
16 oz. unscented and clear glycerin base

Directions:

1. Set up a double boiler on your stove and then add in the glycerin base. Make sure to let this heat up on a low heat setting until the glycerin is completely melted.
2. When the glycerin has had time to melt, add in the other three ingredients and stir to combine well.
3. Bring out the molds that you want to use on this project and pour this soap inside. Place the mold into the fridge so that it has time to set and become hard.
4. When this is done, you can either store the soaps properly until you use them later or use them right away.

Chocolate Cookie Soap

Ingredients:

4 drops brown soap coloring
2 tsp. chocolate oil, fragrance
2 tsp. cocoa butter
16 oz. unscented glycerin base

Directions:

1. To begin this recipe, set up a double boiler on your stove. Add in the glycerin and let it melt down on a medium temperature until it is nice and smooth and melted.
2. Next, pour in the other ingredients and let them mix and combine with the glycerin.
3. Once this is done, choose the molds that you would like to use and then place in the fridge, or another cool spot, to soften for the next 24 hours.
4. Use these soaps right away.

White Cappuccino

Ingredients:

    4 drops white soap coloring
    10 drops coffee oil, fragrance
    2 tsp. milk powder
    16 oz. unscented glycerin base

Directions:

1. Take out a few pots and then set them up as a double boiler on your stove. Add in the glycerin and heat it up slowly until this ingredient has some time to melt.
2. Once the glycerin is melted, add in the rest of the ingredients and stir well.
3. Now pick out the molds you would like to use and pour this soap mixture inside. Allow it to set inside the fridge for the next 24 hours before you take it out and use it for a great bath!

Pink Grapefruit Soap

Ingredients:

    4 drops pink soap coloring
    5 drops grapefruit oil
    ¼ c. coconut oil
    1 Tbsp. aloe vera gel
    1 lb. unscented glycerin base

Directions:

1. Create a double boiler with a few of your pots and then place the glycerin inside along with the coconut oil. Let these melt together until they are smooth.
2. When these are melted, you can add in the rest of the ingredients and stir until they are well combined.
3. When this is all done, take out some molds and pour the soap mixture inside. Let them set inside the fridge for the next 24 hours so it has time to set.
4. Use the soap when it is all done.

Orange Field

Ingredients:

Liquid out of a vitamin E capsule
4 drops orange soap coloring
5 drops orange oil
1 tsp. aloe vera gel
1 Tbsp. coconut oil
1 lb. unscented glycerin base

Directions:

1. Bring out your pots and set up a double boiler that has the coconut oil and glycerin inside. Let them go on a low heat until they have time to melt completely.
2. When these are melted, you can add in the rest of the ingredients, making sure they are completely combined.
3. After this time, bring out the molds that you would like to use and then pour the soap mixture inside.
4. Place these into the fridge to have time to set, about 24 hours, before taking out and using!

Glowing Spring Soap

Ingredients:

    2 drops yellow soap coloring
    8 drops violet leaf oil
    8 drops rosemary oil
    8 drops chamomile oil
    16 oz. unscented glycerin base

Directions:

1. Inside a double boiler, place the glycerin and let it heat up until it is completely melted.
2. Once this is done, take the rest of the ingredients and add them in with the glycerin, mixing to combine together well.
3. At this point, bring out some molds and pour the ingredients inside. Place into the fridge so that they have some time to cool down and set.
4. After this time, take the soaps out of the fridge and then enjoy.

Alluring Orchid

Ingredients:

    4 drops blue soap coloring
    8 drops chamomile oil
    16 oz. vanilla fragrance
    40 drops orchid fragrance
    ¼ c. olive oil
    16 oz. unscented and clear glycerin base

Directions:

1. Bring out two pots and set up a double broiler to use for this step. Place the glycerin base inside and turn to a low heat, allowing to melt the ingredient.
2. When this is completely melted, add in the rest of the ingredients and stir to combine well.
3. When this is done, bring out the molds that you would like to use and then pour the mixture inside. Allow it to set until hardened before using.

Coconut Lime

Ingredients:

- 2 oz. coconut lime fragrance
- 6 oz. safflower oil
- 6 1/3 oz. lye
- 8 oz. sunflower oil
- 14 oz. coconut milk
- 15 oz. olive oil
- 15 oz. coconut oil

Directions:

1. Let the milk freeze for a bit so it becomes a bit slushy. When this is done, place it into a bowl and stir together with the lye before setting aside.
2. Combine together the rest of your ingredients and set it up into a double boiler so they can melt together.
3. Allow your oils and lye to cool down so they end up around 98 degrees. When they are cooled down a bit, add the oils with the lye mix and stir until it becomes like a cake batter.
4. Pour this mix into a mold that you chilled for a bit during this process and then let it set for about 24 hours.
5. Once this is done, the soap needs to be placed into a curing area for at least 3 weeks before using.

CONCLUSION

There are so many reasons why you may choose to make some of your own soaps at home. You will enjoy that it can save you money, that it is easy to do, and that you will be able to pick from way more options than you were able to do before. This is a great process to do at home, even if you are doing it on your own or with someone else to help, and you will soon wonder why you didn't get started on this before.

This guidebook is going to take some time to go over the basics of soap making. It will talk about some of the benefits of doing this in your home along with the main processes that most at home soap makers will use to create the perfect bar of soap. Once you are done learning about the differences in the hot method and the cold method for creating your soaps, it is time to go into the chapter about some of the tools that you will need to make the soaps and a few safety concerns with using lye properly in the mixtures.

Finally this guidebook ends with some of the best recipes that you can use to make some of your own soaps at home. These are simple to make and you will love that there are so many options to use, from the different colors to the scents and everything in between that you can do with your soaps. So when you are tired of being limited at the store for the kinds of soaps that you are able to use and you want to have some more control over the ingredients that go into the soap, and therefore onto your body, take a look through this guidebook and see how easy it is to get started with making some of your own soaps.